# WILLING HANDS

## IN THE SERVICE OF THE LORD

# WILLING HANDS

## IN THE SERVICE OF THE LORD

DAN RICHARD

SQUAREONE PUBLISHERS

EDITOR: Allison Cirruzzo
COVER DESIGNER & TYPESETTER: Jeannie Tudor

**Square One Publishers**
115 Herricks Road
Garden City Park, NY 11040
(516) 535-2010 • (877) 900-BOOK
www.squareonepublishers.com

**Library of Congress Cataloging-in-Publication Data**
Names: Richard, Dan (Lay Minister), author.
Title: Willing hands in the service of the Lord / Dan Richard.
Description: Garden City Park : Square One Publishers, 2018. | Includes bibliographical references and index.
Identifiers: LCCN 2017051552 (print) | LCCN 2017056051 (ebook) | ISBN 0757054617 | ISBN 9780757004612 (pbk. : alk. paper)
Subjects: LCSH: Service (Theology)
Classification: LCC BT738.4 (ebook) | LCC BT738.4 .R53 2018 (print) | DDC 248.4—dc23
LC record available at https://lccn.loc.gov/2017051552



Printed in the United States of America

10 9 8 7 6 5 4 3 2

# Contents

PART 3

## Service within the Church



PART 4

## Service in Sermons

*This small book is dedicated to*
*all who willingly and graciously serve*
*others. You can, and do, make a difference!*
*The world is a better place because of*
*people like you who choose the life of service.*
*Thank you! Thank you! Thank you!*

# Acknowledgments

I would like to recognize those closest to me who have been inspiring, personal examples of service. My dad, Elwood Richard, became a giant in the nutrition industry, but was equally known for his humility, kindness and service to others. He continues to inspire me and remains my greatest mentor and role model. My mom, Betty Richard, served my brother, David, sister, Sharon, and myself for many years when Dad was away from home, working 80+ hour weeks. She quietly cared for our family despite little recognition and she instilled our Christian faith. Thanks indeed Mom!

My wife, Beth, has lived a life of service and really been a helpmate in recent years as we became very involved with refugees. Our life is better because of this life change, and Beth has done more to help others than anyone I know. My children Nathan, Faith and Adam have developed a willing spirit as well. This was essential when the Emena family of ten came to live at our house for almost a month in 2012! Life has never been the same since. That experience led to our eyes being opened to a new way of giving. Thank you to the amazing parents Ramazani and Sangani for their incredible life story and friendship. My life is better for knowing you.

I would like to thank the following people for their insights and wonderful contributions to this project: an anonymous Sister on Chapter 2; Sue Johnson and her mom, Marie, on Chapter 3; Bruce Parker on Chapter 9; Dana Pratt on Chapter 10; Nathan Richard on Chapter 21; and Kari Larsen on Chapter 22.

# Preface

Are you selfish? I am. I really am. I'd much rather serve myself than others, yet God has been working in my life to teach me how, and why, to serve others. It's a journey that all disciples of Jesus must experience and learn. No one is born serving others. Someone who cared enough to raise you had to serve you. Someone had to feed, clothe, change your diaper and care for you. It is only later in life that we learn that service is a choice. We learn to serve because someone served us first.

Writing about service is like describing a beautiful sunset. It's something that has to be experienced in order to be fully appreciated. We choose whether to serve ourselves, or others. We choose whether to serve God or man. We choose whether to serve at home, school, work or play. Service is a choice. It's not the easy road, nor the most natural. We are all naturally selfish and have to change our natural inclinations in order to serve.

Of course the best example of the ideal servant is the Son of Man, Jesus. Everything Jesus did was an act of service to others. He healed. He taught. He fed. He forgave. He loved. He helped. He believed. He cared. He died for you and me. Jesus served in practical and spiritual ways. He understood people's material needs and was sympathetic to all who suffered. "Servant" was actually one of the titles given to Jesus (Isaiah 42:1). He set a high standard when he washed his disciples' feet, just hours before dying on the cross. Jesus "did not come to be served, but to serve and to give his life as ransom for many" (Matthew 20:28).

This book has a variety of subjects intended to help each person's spiritual service. The initial concept was developed in preparation for an adult bible school. That is why there are extra parts for speakers in the church near the end. God willing, something here will connect with you and be helpful in your lifelong walk of service.

Finally, I write these tips primarily as advice to myself, knowing my extensive failings. I hope you can benefit from my faults.

In His Service,
Dan Richard

# Introduction

"Each of you should use whatever gift you have received to serve others, as faithful stewards of God's grace in its various forms."
1 Peter 4:10

You have a purpose in life. You are not an accident. You may not know or understand it fully yet, but you do have a purpose. You have a God-given reason to exist. You were created with a purpose, as part of God's master plan. Your purpose includes a life of service. Really! You were uniquely created to help serve others, and not just yourself.

Did you know that God actually prepares opportunities for you to serve? Yes, the Almighty Creator of all that we know cares enough about you to give you special occasions to help other people. He wants to teach you to become more like Him through service. Hard to believe? In the Bible, the apostle Paul says so: "For we are his workmanship, having been created in Christ Jesus for good works that God prepared beforehand so we may do them" (Ephesians 2:10).

This book has a purpose as well. It is to remind and encourage both Christians and non-Christians of the amazing plan and responsibility to serve. Anyone who helps handicapped children or mentally disabled adults or serves the homeless knows how much they get in return. It feels good to help others. Those who give often receive back much more than expected.

My hope is that you will benefit from the ideas and reminders in this book. The format is intended to be a quick read, and not necessarily all at once. Consider these thoughts as prompts to make service an active part of your life. Service is not easy and we all need help for encouragement and support. Service is a way of life, and a great way of life!

# Original Apostle's Creed

*We believe in God, the Father Almighty,*
*the Maker of heaven and earth,*
*and in Jesus Christ, His only Son, our Lord:*

*Who was conceived by the Holy Spirit,*
*suffered under Pontius Pilate,*
*was crucified, died, and was buried;*

*The third day He arose again from the dead;*

*He ascended into heaven,*
*and sitteth on the right hand of God the Father Almighty;*
*from thence he shall come to judge the quick and the dead.*

*We believe in the communion of saints,*
*the forgiveness of sins,*
*and the resurrection of the body,*
*and life everlasting.*

*Amen.*

# Part 1

## Service Within Your Family

"Love the LORD your God with all your heart
and with all your soul and with all your strength.
These commandments that I give you today are to
be on your hearts. Impress them on your children.
Talk about them when you sit at home and
when you walk along the road, when you
lie down and when you get up."

Deuteronomy 6:5-7

# 1.

# Hospitality 101

"Do not forget to show hospitality to strangers, for by doing so some people have shown hospitality to angels without knowing it."
Hebrews 13:2

Hospitality is becoming a lost art. When was the last time you invited someone to a home-cooked dinner, or welcomed a non-relative to sleep at your house? People don't seem to entertain as much in their homes, even amongst friends. Being hospitable to strangers is even more rare.

Is it any surprise that "hospitality" sounds similar to "hospital?" Both words reflect acts of kindness, short-term accommodation, and generosity towards others. Hospitality is the friendly and generous reception and entertainment of guests, visitors, and strangers. Maybe that's the point of Jesus' parable about the Good Samaritan, who went out of his way, and at considerable expense, to give help and hospitality to a stranger. He reacted to a surprise opportunity to serve and jumped into action.

Jesus was homeless during his ministry, but welcomed all who came to him. He advised, "Whoever welcomes one of these little children in my name welcomes me; and whoever welcomes me does not welcome me but the one who sent me" (Mark 9:37). Disciples of Christ should be hospitable with their homes, time and money if they want to become like Jesus. This should come naturally and not have to feel forced. Jesus raised the bar by suggesting that followers invite the poor, blind and lame to meals instead of friends and family (Luke 14:13).

The apostles learned from Jesus and advised:

- "Share with the Lord's people who are in need. Practice hospitality" (Rom 12:13).
- "Now a bishop is to be above reproach, faithful to his wife…. hospitable" (1 Tim 3:2).
- "Offer hospitality to one another without grumbling" (1 Peter 4:9).
- "We ought therefore to show hospitality to such people" (3 John 8).

*Transform your home into a sanctuary for friends and family with the following suggestions.*

## DO

■ Invite someone over for dinner who you normally would not invite. Be hospitable to strangers like Abraham (Genesis 18).

■ Think of people in need who you can welcome in ways that may make you uncomfortable. This is healthy and good.

■ Make your home like a hospital when it comes to hospitality. Make your home available like an emergency room.

## DON'T

■ Don't give hospitality "grudgingly," but with a cheerful heart.

■ Don't be like Nabal (1 Sam 25) or Diotrephes (3 John 9-10), both of whom were worst-case examples of being inhospitable.

# 2.

# Raising Godly Children

"Children, obey your parents in the Lord, for this is right. 'Honor your father and mother'—which is the first commandment with a promise— 'so that it may go well with you and that you may enjoy long life on the earth.'"
Ephesians 6:1-3

Raising godly children is simple, isn't it? Provide a home full of love and grace, with instruction and discipline, and lots of exposure to the Word. Teach kindness, gentleness and self-control. When those fail, teach repentance, forgiveness, reconciliation and patience. Set appropriate standards for behavior, and deal with poor behavior. Ensure that everyone is well rested and regularly fed. Read the Bible and piles of good books. Gather with believers, formally and informally. Spend time together, having fun. Teach your children how to work. Pray together. Pray for others. Sing hymns. Listen to spiritually uplifting music. Fill your home with goodness and thankfulness.

Sounds simple? It may be simple, but it is not easy! Family life is messy. We encounter sin in our spouses, our children, and ourselves. We may fail to discipline diligently or we discipline too harshly. We love, but we're not always warm. We spend time together, but are easily distracted. The kids argue and seem to hate each other sometimes, and our repeated attempts to turn their hearts are ineffectual. We reach our limits all the time—limits of love and patience and knowledge—as we encounter life's challenges. It is not easy.

We have inherited a factory model mindset where child rearing is reduced to processes and the children themselves are reduced to mere "things" that are molded and produced. We think that if we do the right thing then we can actually make godly children. If the process is predictable, how do we explain Eliab, Manasseh, Nadab and Abihu, Samuel's sons Joel and Abijah, Solomon, and that prodigal son? How do we explain David, Ruth, Rahab, Hezekiah, Josiah, Jonathan, and Samuel's grandson Heman? It's not that we can't have a positive effect on our children—we can—it is that, in the end, the children themselves get to decide. We can't make them decide and

*Encourage and inspire your children to live a full life of faith with the following pointers.*

## DO

- Provide love and grace, discipline and instruction, and exposure to the Word.
- Build relationships based on love and mutual respect, working hard to stay connected.
- Live transparent lives of faith in front of your children.
- Talk to others about the difficulties of parenting.

## DON'T

- See your children as things, objects, possessions, projects, or products.
- Beat yourself up when your children struggle. They will struggle.
- Take credit when your children succeed.
- Isolate. You are not alone in this parenting endeavor.

we can't make the decision for them. We cannot make godly children any more than David could build Solomon's temple. We can provide some raw materials, but the building is their own.

What, then, is our task? We live transparent lives of faith, showing our children what repentance, doubt, love, obedience, praise, lowliness, reliance, joy, honesty, and the relinquishing of the will look like in the life of an imperfect follower of Christ. Watch what I do. Look at how I deal with my sin and your sin. Now watch me love in the face of hatred and reconcile after suffering wrongs. Listen to me pray, for real, from my heart, about real things, to my real God, who is really listening. Watch me read the Word. Join me if you want. This is the path to life. Watch me as I serve. Watch me fail. Watch me as He revives me, again, and yet again. Watch how I spend my time and whose company I seek. Watch me rely on my Lord. Watch me learn that when I am weak, then I am strong. These are our parenting tasks.

In the end, our job is not to make godly children, but to become godly children ourselves—godly children of our Heavenly Father. Do we follow His directions? Do we seek His guidance? Do we love His other children? If we want our children to follow us, then we must become both followers and follow-able. Let us live lives of faith in Him, in front of them, hoping that they will choose to join us.

# 3.

# Caring for an Elderly Parent, Brother, or Sister

"Let us consider how to stimulate one another to love and good deeds, not forsaking our own assembling together, as is the habit of some, but encouraging one another, and all the more,as you see the day drawing near."
Hebrews 10:24-25

Grace and grey hair go together. What a joy it is to build a friendship with someone who has grown wiser in the Lord over many generations! Serving and assisting an elderly parent, brother or sister is really an opportunity for you, too. It is a time to be still, listen, and slow down. Elderly people are often frustrated by the limitations of their flesh, which seem to increase every day. They want to be their old, young selves again but cannot lift things, see things, remember things, or even stay warm the way they used to. One woman told me she has more doctors' appointments every month than she had in her first sixty years of life.

Commit to spending time and listening to them. Many elderly people, who cannot talk clearly, would love for you to read the scriptures to them or sit and hold their hand. Calming music, particularly hymns or harp music, seems to provide comfort for agitated minds. Singing with the person, if they enjoy this, brings a smile. Choose songs they are familiar with.

Exercise is very important, but you will have to discover what your parent or friend enjoys and what their limitations are. How far can they walk? Where would they enjoy walking? Do they enjoy dancing or some group movement class? You will help them sleep better and improve their wellbeing by getting them moving and breathing. Physical contact, like offering a hug and holding their hand, is important to many and especially to those who have lost a spouse. Jesus often healed people with a touch that communicated compassion.

If you decide to have your parent move in with you, it is a good idea to talk about how you will each need to change some of your routines. You are reminding each other to be patient, knowing that feelings of aggravation are normal. If you find yourself assisting during hospice, just be ready to do whatever is necessary. You are the hands of the Lord Jesus as you care for the person. This is a very tender and intimate time and the focus of our faith, as the elder person prepares to fall asleep in the Lord, awaiting the resurrection of the dead!

*The following guidelines will help you in serving your elderly parent, sibling, friend, or other relative.*

## DO

■ Read the Bible everyday to focus on what is important.

■ Listen. Listen. Listen.

## DON'T

■ Be impatient. Remember that this may be the highest calling in your life of service.

■ Avoid difficult conversations. Be sure to know what choices your parent wants ahead of time regarding their declining health and, eventually, funeral services.

# 4.

# Serving Your Spouse

"The man said, 'This is now bone of my bones and flesh of my flesh; she shall be called 'woman', for she was taken out of man.' That is why a man leaves his father and mother and is united to his wife, and they become one flesh."

Genesis 2:23-2

Let's face it: sometimes the last thing we want to do is serve our husband or wife. Just the idea may seem offensive and unfair. Being married "happily ever after" is a pipe dream for too many Christians. With half of all marriages ending in divorce and many more existing in an unhealthy state, it is a major challenge to have a spiritually successful marriage. Yet that is what we are called to do.

Adam was first blessed to have Eve as his wife and helpmate. God provided the state of marriage for man and woman to ease the problem of loneliness. No other animal or relationship would do. Paul later gave Godly advice to married people (1 Cor. 7) regarding self-control, commitment, and marriage responsibilities. He gave perhaps his best advice in Ephesians 5, when he wrote how wives should submit to their husbands and husbands should love their wives. But that directive was preceded with the most important passage we tend to forget: "Submit to one another out of reverence for Christ." Both the husband and wife are exhorted to submit to each other, it's not just the wife who is called to submit!

Aquila and Priscilla were one of the best examples of a Godly marriage. They worked together as tent-makers with Paul, and they wisely corrected Apollos about one misbelief (Acts 18). We get enough insight in Acts to learn that these disciples served each other daily, as they did to others.

Some practical ways to serve our spouse are found in *The Five Love Languages*, by Gary Chapman. He identifies primary "love languages" that people must learn to speak if they want a healthy marriage. These include Words of Affirmation, Quality Time, Gifts, Acts of Service, and Physical Affection. Each of these "languages" may be foreign to you and me, but we have to find ways to serve our spouse in ways that they value. Do you know which love language is most important to your spouse? Do you remember how you wanted to serve your spouse when you were first dating? Wouldn't it be healthy to renew that feeling, and action? Your personal happiness and spiritual survival will likely depend on how you successfully serve your spouse.

*Uphold your duties as a loving, reverent spouse with the following suggestions.*

## DO

■ Take the initiative to serve your spouse with little things. Help with dishes, laundry, cleaning and errands. Be the first to deal with problems with your children.

■ Find out what makes your spouse feel good. We all remember who, and what, makes us feel better. Commit to serving your spouse, even if you don't want to.

## DON'T

■ Blame your spouse for your marriage problems. Assume issues are your fault and your own spiritual failing first. Then seek God's help.

■ Give up. Get help from a friend or counselor. Learning to be selfless to your spouse is a lifelong pursuit.

# 5.

# Serving at Home

"Choose for yourselves this day whom you will serve ... But as for me and my household, we will serve the LORD."

Joshua 24:15

Every family is dysfunctional to some degree. The outward signs are apparent to all: Isolation, judgment, conflict, neglect, unkindness, lack of respect, distrust, gossip, guilt and abuse. It's unnatural to serve family members when part of an unhealthy relationship. King David was "a man after God's own heart," yet he led a seriously dysfunctional family filled with rape, murder, orgy, discord, factions, rebellion and capital punishment. David was a great leader to the nation of Israel, but a lousy father servant to his family.

Every family member can serve at home. Volunteering to do chores. Using your kitchen as a base to prepare meals for elderly, sick or new moms. Writing real paper cards or letters of encouragement. Practicing piano lessons to serve at church. Praying before meals. Doing family bible readings together. Host a bible class or home church. Being hospitable. Consciously using time and resources wisely to serve others.

People used their homes in the Bible to serve in various ways. Abraham used his tent home to welcome and feed angels. A Shunammite woman (2 Kings 4) provided for the prophet Elisha's needs. An unknown disciple provided a private home and Passover meal for Jesus and the twelve apostles. Paul leaned on various helpers for meals, housing and physical care. None are exempt from the ability or responsibility to serve others within their homes.

The supernatural woman in Proverbs 31 is an amazing example. She manages to do it all, setting the bar impossibly high. She serves her family 100 percent, while working hard both at home, and away from home. She works with her hands and prepares food for her family. She is a production worker, merchant, banker, and manager all rolled into one. She has no time for idleness, but rises early each day to lead her family. She is selfless in everything she does.

*Foster a loving, godly family dynamic within your home with the following tips.*

## DO

■ Think of things you can volunteer to do within your home and family. Make a list and start doing.

■ Eat meals together and plan quality time together. Limit time wasters like TV, video games, Facebook and selfish pursuits.

■ Create a welcoming and Christ-like atmosphere in your home that others will want to model after.

## DON'T

■ Don't minimize the quantity and quality of your family time. Both are essential to serving your family.

■ Never be a stranger to your family. Don't let your kids grow up with you as their absentee parent. See Psalm 69:8.

# Part 2

## Service Within the Community

# 6.

# Welcoming Refugees

"The stranger who dwells among you shall be to you as one born among you, and you shall love him as yourself; for you were strangers in the land of Egypt: I am the LORD your God."

Leviticus 19:34

Centuries ago, our ancestors traveled long voyages overseas to settle here in America. Few Americans today are truly Native. Our country's welcome mat at the Statue of Liberty famously reads, "Give me your tired, your poor, your huddled masses yearning to breathe free, the wretched refuse of your teeming shore. Send these, the homeless, tempest-tossed to me, I lift my lamp beside the golden door!" It is a reminder that the world is changing and the need is greater than ever to seek out and help refugees. We should welcome all who seek refuge here, as our ancestors did long ago.

The Bible is full of those who are called strangers, sojourners, foreigners, homeless and alien. Abraham, Isaac, Jacob, Joseph, Ruth, Uriah, and Jeremiah are but a few. The Children of Israel were themselves slaves and refugees in Egypt, which is why the law commanded them to care for others when they had their own homes. In fact, all the Faithful listed in the Hall of Faith chapter were considered strangers or refugees (Heb 11:13). Jesus directed his followers to welcome and care for strangers (Matt 25:35). Paul repeated the same (1 Tim 5:10; Heb 13:2). Jesus was a refugee himself when his family fled from Herod to seek refuge in Egypt. We should be sensitive to help refugees because the Christian's true citizenship is in heaven, and not in the country we reside. That means that you are a refugee too!

There are so many ways to help. Find a family or individuals who are fairly new to the country. Ask how you can help. Get involved. Simple tasks to you may be like a foreign language to someone else. Think about what you would need if you were forced from your home with no notice and lived as a homeless family. You would need help with basics such as food, clothing, and shelter. You might also need help finding a job to provide for your family and learning how to drive. Most of all, you would need a friend to help you figure out your new life and get settled into new habits. It's amazing how many daily things we take for granted, which many refugees need to survive.

*Helping refugees may be the most rewarding work that you ever do. Consider these hints below:*

## DO

■ Volunteer directly or indirectly through a refugee service.

■ Expect to give of yourself in unexpected ways, and always be flexible. Pray for refugees' welfare.

■ Be patient. Learn to ask others how to help. You may need to learn how to navigate insurance, health care, schools, ESL classes, charities, housing, and search for a viable job.

## DON'T

■ Assume your culture, language, foods, or traditions are superior to refugees. You can greatly help someone integrate into a new society.

■ Create dependency. Teach refugees to fish. They need to move away from government handouts and towards contributing to church and society.

# 7.

# Feed My Starving Children

"There are different kinds of service, but the same Lord. There are different kinds of working, but in all of them and in everyone it is the same God at work."
1 Corinthians 12:5-6

Founded in 1992, Make-a-Difference Day is a national service day that encourages Americans to be more charitable with their time and money. There are many other group service days just like it, including National Volunteer Day, International Volunteer Day, and Global Youth Service Day. These are all good efforts to motivate people to help with community cleanups, donate blood, cook a meal for someone in need, help a food pantry or physically work with a group like Habitat for Humanity.

A sister in our church organized a volunteer group to work for a few hours for a charity called Feed My Starving Children (www.fmsc.org). This non-profit is one of many that serve a great need with this mission: "Blessed are those who are generous, because they feed the poor" (Prov 22:9). All who participated said that the experience made them feel better and connected to the mission of that charity. It also helped the church members to work together, including with some who had not been attending services lately.

The Bible is full of examples and direction to serve one another. Paul advised that you "show yourself to be an example of good deeds" and "Our people must also learn to engage in good deeds to meet pressing needs, so that they will not be unfruitful" (Titus 3:14). There are many charities today that would appreciate you volunteering to help their cause. A Christian can be an active supporter of any number of social charities as well as donating time and money to their local church.

Jesus set the standard for serving others. He fed strangers both literally and spiritually. He saw practical needs and reached out to help those he encountered. Jesus lived a life where he actually made a difference in lives every single day. Our challenge is to do the same. We are called to make a difference in people around us. We are called to assertively find ways where we can help those in need. We are called to be more like Jesus in serving others.

*Doing volunteer work is a wonderful way to serve your community.*

## DO

■ Look for ways that you can volunteer your time and energy in your community. Service is a choice where you need to act like a servant. Think on these things. (Phil 4:8)

■ Pray for God to give you opportunities to help others. He will, so be ready!

■ See if you can find a buddy to volunteer with. This will help encourage you in your service and make the time more enjoyable.

## DON'T

■ Think that donating your time outside your church is worth less than church activities. We know that faith without works is dead, so try to improve in both areas.

■ Think thoughts like "the poor you will always have with you" as an excuse to do nothing. Helping just one person can make a big difference for them.

# 8.

# Service at Your Workplace

"Continue to work out your salvation with fear and trembling, for it is God who works in you to will and to act in order to fulfill his good purpose."
Phil 2:12-13

The time you spend at work is not a curse to be endured. It also should not be a hidden, disconnected part of your Christian life. Work is a gift from God, first given to Adam and Eve before sin entered the world. Whether your work is at the office, in the factory, on the road or at home, you have a great opportunity to show Christian service at work.

It would be a sad commentary if your co-workers assumed you are not a Christian because of how you work. That would happen if you were a poor quality worker. Or a worker with a bad attitude. Or a worker who only worked hard when the boss is looking. Or a worker who did the least possible work in order to just get by. That's the opposite of what is known as a "Christian work ethic." As a model worker, Paul gave this practical advice: "Whatever you do, work at it with all your heart, as working for the Lord" (Colossians 3:23).

The Bible gives plenty of guidance for being a good servant at work. Joseph was a hard and loyal worker, recognized by his boss, and blessed by God. Ruth worked tirelessly to provide for her household, and she received a handsome reward, literally! Nehemiah organized a team of workers and they built a major wall in record time. Even Jesus grew up as a carpenter, learning a trade, and surely supporting his family with physical work.

We are told to be content with our work because it is the gift of God. Joni Eareckson Tada is a Christian musician who happens to be a quadriplegic. She sings an amazing song about how she wishes that she could experience the joy of washing the dishes, doing laundry and changing a diaper. That is the attitude Christians should strive to follow. The mindset of joy, honesty, thankfulness, helpfulness and willing service is what drives a Christian to be the best worker and co-worker. Again, Paul writes: "For we are His workmanship, created in Christ Jesus for good works, which God prepared beforehand so that we would walk in them" (Ephesians 3:10).

*Maintain a proper Christian work ethic and keep a positive attitude towards your work with the following tips.*

## DO

■ Practice being a honest, hard worker. Paul worked "day and night" as an example for us (1 Thes 2:9). Your primary service at work is to your boss or owner.

■ Think of ways where you can serve co-workers. People have many needs and you have opportunities to help when you talk and listen to their work or home needs.

## DON'T

■ Gossip at work and don't avoid doing "the dirty work."

■ Be satisfied with poor quality work. You serve customers and should "Do unto others as you would have them do unto you."

■ Join a union unless necessary. Going on strike is a contrary position for a Christian who should be content with work and wages (Luke 3:14).

# 9.

# Serving in the Mission Field

"I am on my way to Jerusalem in the service of the Lord's people there."
Romans 15:25

"Mission" may be a multi-year commitment in India, Africa or Latin America, or a week or month during holidays serving others, with God's word and God's grace. The first goal of mission is to serve. To know yourself and find the right way to use your gifts for God is challenging. Prayer is vital. Networking with those more experienced can help avoid mistakes. A second goal of mission is to grow: to mature personally, learning to express God's love. Your example should draw others to God and his Son. It won't happen if you are arrogant or patronizing. Do what you are asked to do.

There are known pitfalls. One is culture shock due to what we encounter in the field. Often just as shocking is the transition home after your mission. This can be reduced with preparation and suitable counseling. Also, going on mission alone or with a friend may seem like fun, but without proper guidance and physical/spiritual/emotional support, may be a recipe for disaster.

If God is guiding you to serve, it will come about naturally as you explore options. People who know you well may encourage you to find other ways to serve. The mission field is not for everyone. Don't force it, as though it were a box to be checked in your spiritual journey. Nor is mission service a guarantor of future spiritual strength. It becomes what you make of it prayerfully, with suitable guidance and support. Mission doesn't end when you return home. Maybe it really begins then. May God motivate and guide your willing service.

*Take on a mission of your own—big or small—with the following guidance.*

## DO

■ Pray, and prepare Biblically. Don't wait to reach the 'field' to commit to daily time in the Word and in prayer.

■ Get good advice from those who have gone before. Be sure you will have good emotional and spiritual support while there.

■ Go to be an agent of God's love and compassion. Be flexible; it never looks like you imagined.

## DON'T

■ Go for a holiday and call it a mission... a tourist is not a missionary, and vice-versa.

■ Forget to learn as well as teach, accept guidance and help.

■ Go into physically or emotionally challenging situations if you have a history of being fragile in those ways. Find another way to serve.

■ Get so busy with mission 'stuff' that you lose your daily 'God' time and try not to be discouraged. May God motivate and guide your willing service.

# 10.

# Teaching English as a Second Language

"Each one should use whatever gift he has received to serve others, faithfully administering God's grace in its various forms."
1 Peter 4:10

The children of Israel were commanded over and over to treat the foreigners among them with kindness (Deut 10:19). God used this command to remind them that their patriarchs were once foreigners in the land of Canaan. He also frequently brings up the fact that they were "strangers" in the Land of Egypt, and therefore should not oppress or do wrong toward such people who might choose to dwell in their nation. He wanted them to have hearts of service and compassion toward the alien in their midst.

There are so many simple things that we take for granted that are very difficult for people who do not have good English skills in an English-speaking country. Churches can offer courses in teaching English as a Second Language (ESL) to give tangible help to people who are working hard to make their way in a new country. Offering this as a free service is very helpful to folks who may have limited incomes or not be able to attend frequent classes at local colleges.

Teaching English in a formal way is not as complicated as it may seem. It involves discerning the level of input the person is capable of receiving and helping them practice skills over and over. The Bible is a great resource for developing reading and comprehension lessons. Often the people from other countries have had little or no exposure to the stories of the Bible and they find it interesting and motivating. As relationships are built over time, some of the students will inevitably become interested in pursuing more in depth Bible lessons and possibly even baptism.

There are great online resources for developing lessons and review exercises. One of the best is the ESL Library at ESL-library.com. This is a subscription site, but membership allows all in the church to have access to over 700 lessons designed for professional English teachers. It is full of excellent tools like interactive exercises, flashcards, and American culture lessons at Beginner, Intermediate, and Advanced levels. Other resources that are helpful include flannel graph boards to help convey the Bible stories, Children's Bible storybooks, Sunday school lesson sites, and other online resources. Hands-on learning (like cooking together and using that experience to generate vocabulary) is always fun and welcome. Hospitality offered to the students outside of the class is also a great way to strengthen relationships. Surely this is something God finds pleasing in His children.

*Be a successful ESL teacher and help others learn with the following tips.*

## DO

■ Your homework online and ask others with experience teaching ESL for guidance.

■ Plan your time availability to make sure you can commit to a regular schedule. Helping to teach English is a long-term time commitment.

## DON'T

■ Try to teach without using professional resources. Most of us are not experienced with this and it makes sense to tap into what works for others.

■ Assume this is too easy or too hard. You can do this, and the positive feelings can be so rewarding.

# 11.

# Serving in Preaching

"And my message and my preaching were very plain. Rather than using clever and persuasive speeches, I relied only on the power of the Holy Spirit."
1 Corinthians 2:4

Many people save lives today. Nurses, firemen, police officers save lives. Drug rehab institutions save lives. School counselors save lives. Paramedics save lives. Homeless advocates save lives. Here's a radical thought: Preachers save lives, too. Eternal lives.

Preaching gets a bad rap today. Our culture says that preaching is judging and politically incorrect because it offends people. Yet the Bible clearly tells disciples of Jesus to "preach the word, in season and out of season." We are called to follow in the footsteps of Old Testament prophets like Moses, Elijah, Isaiah, Jeremiah, and Jonah. Each of these prophets had missions to preach to their people and declare God's will. Later, John the Baptist became the greatest of all born of women, because he was a great preacher who prepared the way of his Lord.

Ezekiel had a special calling to be a watchman, or preacher, to his people. God warned him how important the watchman is, and how much responsibility he bears. Lives depended on the watchman blowing the trumpet to warn of enemies. If he failed to warn the people, he would be held responsible for their blood (Ezekiel 33:1-11). In the same way, followers of Jesus must declare what they know to be true. We have a job to communicate to people around us the good news of the Kingdom of God and the name of Jesus Christ (Acts 8:12).

So why do we preach? We preach because we are commanded to preach. We want to save lives and "how can they hear without someone preaching to them?" (Rom 10:14) We preach because preaching is an act of God and it's not about us. We preach because we know. We preach because Jesus preached and we want to be like Jesus.

*Preach for success with the suggestions below.*

## DO

■ Preach with and without your words. As Francis of Assisi said, "It is no use walking anywhere to preach unless our walking is our preaching." Practice what you preach.

■ Make a plan to preach, write it down and ask other disciples to help.

■ As Paul said, "Until I come, devote yourself to the public reading of Scripture, to preaching and to teaching" (1 Timothy 4:13).

## DON'T

■ Make excuses why not to preach. It's not spiritually healthy and not like Christ. Preach even when you don't want to.

■ Just condemn others, preach the good news of the Kingdom of God and offer this dark world hope.

■ Try to preach once and then give up. Your friends and family's eternal lives may depend on you being a Preacher of Righteousness.

# 12.

# Serving the Disabled

"So in everything, do to others what you would have them do to you, for this sums up the Law and the Prophets."

Matthew 7:12

The statistics are staggering. Over 10 percent of the world population is disabled. One in sixty-eight American children are now identified as having autism spectrum disorder (ASD). Millions have severe disabilities that require professional long-term care. Disabilities include aging population ailments, malnutrition, injuries, disease, genetic defects and effects of violence. It's no surprise that disabled people are less employed, have more poverty, less education and more depression. Disabled people need your help.

The Bible uses the term "helpless" or "needy" to describe those who need help just to survive. Moses directed the Children of Israel to care for the needy by giving them justice, timely wages, free leftover food and charity (Deut 24). We are told to "Speak up for those who cannot speak for themselves, for the rights of all who are destitute (Prov 31:8). The Psalms are filled with words of comfort describing how our Creator is the ultimate helper of the helpless.

Jesus went out of his way to show compassion on the severely disabled. He healed the blind, lame, deaf, and mute. He must have been amazed when four friends made a Herculean effort to carry a lame man through the roof and into his presence in order to be healed. Their faithful act made a major difference in the life of that man (Mark 2). Peter and John gave us an example when they encountered a lame man who was begging. They couldn't give silver or gold, but they gave that man what they could.

The real lesson to those who are healthy is that we are the ones who are truly helpless. Without Jesus, none of us would be anything; "For while we were still helpless, at the right time Christ died for the ungodly" (Romans 5:6). Each one of us should serve the disabled among us because we have been served by Jesus. If we want to be more like Jesus, we should be the Good Samaritan in someone else's life.

*Give aid to the disabled with the tips below.*

## DO

■ Communicate directly to disabled people and ask how you can help. Don't be offended if some people do not accept your offer for help.

■ Be respectful in your communication and try to be as normal as possible.

■ Seek out volunteer opportunities or donate directly to a needy, disabled person.

## DON'T

■ "Talk down" to anyone with a disability. We all need a little help at times.

■ Offer medical advice, the disabled person likely knows a lot more about their problem than you do.

# 13.

# Serving as Youth

"Let no one look down on your youthfulness, but rather in speech, conduct, love, faith and purity, show yourself an example of those who believe."
1 Timothy 4:12

We need you. Yes, you. The church needs young people to develop, contribute and prepare to lead the next generation. Young people are especially suited to bring fresh ideas and energy to help keep the church alive and relevant. Older members can get too comfortable doing the same old things, and need the questions and prompts that naturally flow from young people.

Young people seem to be naturally good at service in some ways. They are often the first volunteers to participate in a group service project like feeding homeless people, helping a family move homes or go on mission trips. Young people are also more likely to share their faith without hesitation, with less concern for embarrassment or rejection.

There are some incredibly faithful youths in the Bible. Joseph was an amazing seventeen-year-old who did what his father asked, despite the known dangers from his own brothers. He survived, and thrived, in Egypt while always remembering his divine, youthful dreams. David believed that he was a child of promise and took on a giant he really had no business fighting. Josiah was a unique sixteen-year-old who did right in the sight of God by cleansing and reviving the nation. Jeremiah was a youth when first called, and he began a long ministry combating the sins of his people. Daniel was the cream-of-the-crop among his young people and he challenged the command of the king in order to remain faithful to his God.

Jesus once asked Peter, "Do you love me more than these?" He asks the same question of each of us today, including young people. When you make decisions, do you consider if you love Jesus more than your girlfriend, job, school, or friends? Do you make plans to serve others with Jesus in mind? Do you intently make time to serve others? A wise man once said, "Remember your creator in the days of your youth, before the days of trouble come, and the years draw near when you will say, "I have no pleasure in them" (Ecclesiastes 12:1).

*Begin your life of service with the following pointers.*

## DO

■ Volunteer and try different service projects. You don't need to travel great distances to serve. Opportunities are everywhere.

■ Study how Jesus served and seek to be more like Jesus in your daily life.

■ Be a positive example for your friends, and even church elders. You can make an amazing difference in others by doing good.

## DON'T

■ Serve with the goal of gaining Kingdom points. Serve because others have served you first. Serve because Jesus served.

■ Wait to be asked to serve. Volunteer when you see a need, or ask if there is a need you can help serve.

# 14.

# Service in Retirement

"It is the LORD your God you must follow, and him you must revere. Keep his commands and obey him; serve him and hold fast to him."
Deuteronomy 13:4

Aging gracefully is a work in progress. Some people "retire" at a certain age and plan to rest and relax from many years of scheduled work. Others plan to play golf daily, or travel the world, or spend extensive time on hobbies. That might sound good to younger people, but many seniors are dissatisfied with their lives. Loneliness, declining physical and mental health, and depression are real issues that limit many seniors' happiness.

Productive life should not end when a person "retires." Extra unscheduled time allows older people the opportunity to serve others in unique ways. Seniors have significant experience and wisdom that can benefit the next generation. Some people develop a second, part-time career mentoring family, friends, and strangers. Elders can share Godly advice on marriage, child rearing, finances, relationships, careers, and much more. Seniors have talents that are desperately needed by today's younger generation.

In the Bible, many elderly men and women did amazing things. Moses was eighty years old when God called him to lead the Israelites out of Egypt and he continued leading and teaching for forty more years. Abraham was a hundred years old when his ninety-year-old wife, Sarah, had a special promised son, Isaac. Abraham's accomplishments after this age are incredible. He negotiated with God, acted as prophet, obeyed God in travels, was a widow, remarried, took care to find a wife for Isaac, and divided his fortune among his sons. Abraham didn't seem to slow down one bit despite his age!

Scriptures are full of many more "senior citizens" who were leaders of Israel. Isaac, Jacob, Joshua, Caleb, Samuel, and most of the prophets did their most noteworthy work after our retirement age. When Jesus was born, Anna and Simeon (Luke 2) were both mentioned for their righteousness in their old age. Paul described himself as "an old man" in his letter to Philemon and his work wasn't done yet!

*The following suggestions will help you be a faithful servant in retirement.*

## DO

■ Volunteer at non-profits such as your local food pantry or Meals-on-Wheels. Visit shut-ins or cook for those in need.

■ If you are homebound, don't give up. You can serve others by mailing cards to sick people or connecting on social networks.

■ Look for ways to mentor young people. Elders have vast experiences that are valuable for young people. Start with your grandchildren and spend quality time together. Attend whatever events they do to connect and support.

## DON'T

■ Fall into a non-productive routine. You will be healthier and happier when you are actively serving others.

■ Let your weaknesses (health, memory, energy…) limit you. Everyone has more potential than we realize.

# Part 3

## Service Within the Church

"Be dressed ready for service and keep your lamps burning, like servants waiting for their master to return from a wedding banquet, so that when he comes and knocks they can immediately open the door for him."

Luke 12:35-36

# 15.

# Serving by Attendance *Just Show Up*

"Whoever heard me spoke well of me, and those who saw me commended me, because I rescued the poor who cried for help, and the fatherless who had none to assist them."

Job 29:11-12

Sales people have a bag full of tricks to help sell their goods. Some have electric personalities; others use liberal samples or slick literature; some focus on presentation skills or persuasive abilities. But one successful sales rule is simple and universal: Just show up. 80 percent of the sales job is showing up. In sales, that means going through the motions of making the appropriate phone calls, communicating by e-mail, and personal visits. A salesperson cannot do their job without going through these basic motions. Of course, the sales rep must do the basics of presenting their product courteously without being too pushy. But the basic requirement is to just be there and make the sales calls.

Spiritually, we have a higher calling to "just show up" to cover our spiritual basics. That means attending church for memorial service and Sunday school every week, faithfully being at Bible class, reading our Bible daily, praying as we ought, and opening our mouths to share our faith. Who can draw near to God if they don't listen to him? Or who can avoid starving spiritually if regular spiritual food is not ingested? In addition to doing things for our own benefit, we have a responsibility to go to church functions and help others. Every part of the church body is essential—that's what Paul told us (1 Corinthians 12). We need to show up to show care for one another.

*Fulfilling your spiritual duties is easy with the following tips.*

## DO

■ Make it your life habit to read God's word every day. Your life depends on it.

■ Attending church and Sunday school should be obvious norms. Be sure to attend a local bible study as well if you are able.

■ Pray when you feel like it. Pray when you don't feel like it. Pray until you feel like it.

■ Ask yourself in what spiritual areas you could, or should, just show up

## DON'T

■ Sit back and wait for others to volunteer instead of you. God has called you to active discipleship.

■ Justify activities that keep you from showing up at "your reasonable service."

■ Do good works to go through the motions. Do good, as Jesus did.

■ Assume no one cares if you do not show up. People notice, and care.

Jehoshaphat was the King of Judah when the Ammonites and Moabites were enemies and about to attack. Jehoshaphat prayed sincerely and God answered by telling him to have his army simply show up and watch God deliver the nation. Moses exhorted the people of Israel in the same way to "Stand still and see the salvation of the Lord." All they had to do was show up and believe. They did, and God delivered His people by dividing the Red Sea. Thomas was rewarded as well when, while still unbelieving, he continued to attend with the apostles and he saw his risen Lord (John 20). He would not have experienced his greatest joy if he had failed to just show up.

# 16.

# "How can I help you?" Attitude of Service

"I will seek out the lost, bring back the strays, bind up the wounded, and strengthen the weak."

Ezekiel 34:16

There are givers and takers in life and it's pretty obvious who is who. Some people are gifted with Acts of Service as their love language. These people think about helping others without needing to be prompted. They come in all faiths and truly give of themselves to help others. The world is certainly a better place because of givers. The rest of us need to work at serving and consciously try to do what is right. We are naturally selfish and putting others' interests first takes a lot of effort. Can you remember the last special act of service that you did for someone else? Hopefully there are too many to count, but for most of us we need a nudge to try to think naturally about helping others.

Jonathan, son of Saul, had an amazing heart for service. He grew up privileged as the first-born son of the king. He was in line to be the next king of Israel and was a mighty man of valor in his own right. Yet Jonathan did everything in his power to serve David and not himself. He helped David in his greatest times of need—knowing that this would mean losing the throne. Jonathan gave David his robe, tunic, sword, bow and belt—pretty much everything a warrior and future king would need. Jonathan was also an amazing peacemaker as he tried to serve his Father, while also serving his best friend, David. There isn't one negative word recorded about Jonathan, because he had a servant's heart for service.

The Bible is full of minor characters who helped others and served with an attitude of gratitude. In the New Testament, Paul had a small army of helpers who assisted him with physical support, travels, funding and care. We read of Luke, Timothy, Erastus, Aquila and Priscilla, Silas, Barnabas, John, and so many more who were necessary helpers for Paul's ministry. Romans 16 is full of many more who were faithful in assisting Paul.

Jesus was the ultimate servant with the attitude to help and serve others. Jesus sacrificed his time, his energy, his family, his friendships, his future plans, and ultimately his life. Our high calling is to be like Him. Our entire discipleship is an effort to follow our Master—in his service.

*Maintain a positive attitude of service with the suggestions below.*

## DO

■ Ask often, "How can I help you?" Realize that service is a choice and an attitude.

■ Remind yourself that you serve the Lord when you serve his servants.

■ If your gift is serving, then serve. (Rom 12:7) If not, then learn to serve.

## DON'T

■ Serve in order to earn "kingdom points." Serve to be more like Jesus.

■ Brag about your service, that is self-defeating. (Matt 6)

■ Serve begrudgingly. Serve gladly and be a cheerful giver.

# 17.

# Operation—Lost Sheep, Inside the Church

"My people have become lost sheep; their shepherds have led them astray. They have made them turn aside... and have forgotten their resting place."
Jeremiah 50:6

Jesus sure knew how to tell a story. In Luke 15, we read of three parables about someone or something that is lost. Each is designed to show how our Heavenly Father feels about his wayward children. He takes no pleasure in the death of the wicked. God wants to reward his children who diligently seek Him. He wants us to show faithful obedience, and not to be hypocrites. One parable Jesus spoke about involved a woman with ten coins. She lost one coin inside the house and searched carefully until she found it. Notice how this is inside the house. For us, Jesus is talking about people being lost within the church today.

We all get lost within the church at some point in our lives. Even the Psalmist who loved the law of the Lord so much found himself lost and in need of a Shepherd (Ps 119:176). We see church members who are less connected, whose attendance is slacking, who seem disinterested on Sunday. Maybe someone offended them and they hold a grudge. Or maybe the challenges of life have weakened their faith. Everyone sees the elephant in the room, but few reach out to help. It must be someone else's job, right? What would they say anyway? What would you say?

According to Barna research, 59 percent of 19 to 29 year olds leave the Christian church today. That's a sad and scary number. Young people say that the reason they leave churches is largely because the church didn't connect with them. The ones that leave are telling us, "You lost me!" If our young people don't remain faithful, then who will be our future church leaders? We need to devote much more attention to building up our Sunday school classes, and not just for children. We need to seek out those who are lost within our church today.

What would you do differently if you knew someone at your church was attending for the last time? Wouldn't you make a superhuman effort to do everything within your power to help? Jesus came to seek and to save those who are lost, both inside, and outside the church. We should too.

*Offer guidance and support to those feeling a little lost inside the church with the following tips.*

## DO

- Be aware of other church members' needs.
- Get connected at church, and socialize outside Sunday morning.
- Take responsibility to help those who are lost within the church. At some point you'll need someone else to help you.
- Stay within the church fold yourself. The grass is not greener outside. Be faithful.

## DON'T

- Make anyone's problems worse. Bear one another's burdens and so fulfill the law of Christ (Gal 6:2).
- Assume someone else will help someone. It's your responsibility too.
- Be dissuaded from encouraging young people, and don't judge them over the small stuff.

# 18.

# Operation—Lost Sheep, Outside the Church

"Whoever serves me must follow me; and where I am, my servant also will be. My Father will honor the one who serves me."

John 12:26

Unfortunately, most of us know someone well who stopped attending church and "lost their faith." They tell us that they no longer believe the things they used to and that we should leave them alone and not be judgmental. So what should we do? Should we mind our own business and avoid the subject? Should we ask someone else to help? Should we pray? Should we say something, and what? Jesus told the parable about a man who has a hundred sheep and one of them goes astray (Luke 15:4-7). He leaves the ninety-nine sheep in the open pasture and seeks to find the one sheep that is lost, until he finds it! The Good Shepherd never gives up searching. He risks leaving the ninety-nine "safe" sheep because the one sheep is so important. It's a matter of life and death. The lost sheep will not live for long outside the safety of the fold, and under the care of the Good Shepherd.

Jesus knew this too well, as he taught his disciples to "go to the lost sheep of the house of Israel" as their primary mission. They were directed to first call the sinners, not the righteous, because they had the greatest need. Every believer has the responsibility to help recover lost sheep. It's not something that we are allowed to dismiss or avoid. It is a life-and-death matter and has to have our full attention and urgency. We might appreciate the importance more if we were the ones with our life in doubt and we needed someone else to intervene. Many of us can relate to this since someone likely helped save our life at some point. Each disciple of Christ must seek out ways where we can help save a life, especially those who are closest to our reach.

The main point is to never give up seeking to save a child of God who is lost. "All of us like sheep have gone astray, each of us has turned to his own way" (Is 53:6). We can relate because we are sinners as well and we all need a spiritual hospital at some point in our lives. Make sure you and your church are overly welcoming to former members and not cold, judgmental or unwelcoming. "Let him know that he who turns a sinner from the error of his way will save his soul from death, and will cover a multitude of sins" (James 5:20).

*Offer guidance and support to those feeling a little lost outside the church with the following tips.*

## DO

■ Seek out people who have lost their faith. Make a list and start to take action. Ask for help if you are unable to reach a person too close or too far from your social circle.

■ Consider ways to connect socially with former church members. This may be the best way to encourage people without being judgmental or "bossy."

■ Always pray for lost sheep. Prayer can move mountains, and the Good Shepherd still cares today for the one.

## DON'T

■ Fail to do anything.This really is a matter of life and death and this is part of your high calling.

■ Make a former member feel guilty or blame anyone. People problems are normally the main problem why people stop practicing their faith at church.

■ Give up! Keep trying practical ways to help anyone lost outside the church.

# 19.

# Financial Service

"Whoever can be trusted with very little can also be trusted with much, and whoever is dishonest with very little will also be dishonest with much. So if you have not been trustworthy n handling worldly wealth, who will trust you with true riches?"

Luke 16:10-11

According to the IRS, the highest charitable givers are both high and low-income earners. The middle class, surprisingly, donates the lowest percent of total income (2.6 percent). Religious people donate about twice as much to their causes, yet no group of people in the US donates more than 4 percent of their total gross income! Sad, but true. Christians may feel, or claim, to be generous with donations, but in general most of us need to rethink how much we donate to our church.

The Biblical model of tithing began with Abraham and continued throughout the Old Testament (Lev 27:30-32; Numb 18:21-28; Deut 12:6-17; Deut 14:22-28 and 2 Chron 31:5-12). The expectation for Israel was for each person to give 10 percent of their earnings to the priests to provide for various sacrifice offerings. The prophets Haggai and Malachi both appealed to the people to give the equivalent of their first fruits. Sacrificing blind or lame animals did not meet the high standard that Abraham and David set generations earlier (2 Sam 24:24).

Jesus raised the standard of giving when he praised the poor widow who donated two small copper coins (Luke 21:1-4). She barely owned a thing, and yet she gave "all that she had". Jesus taught us to share with whoever asks us, as well as to give privately, so that no one else sees how generous you are. He even sent his disciples out to preach, help, heal and drive out demons—all without taking any payment. Jesus showed us that it is more blessed to give than to receive.

How are you doing with your financial giving? Do you find ways to justify not giving what you should? Are you a generous, cheerful giver? Many people are able to donate their time and physical help, which is a good thing. We should donate financially to our local church especially, since that is where we are fed spiritually. There are many other godly charities that are worthy to be supported financially, as well as with time and energy.

*Find ways to give charitably to those in need by following the tips below.*

## DO

■ Consider donating financially more than you do today. If you're like most Christians, you could do more. "The love of money is the root of all evil."

■ Be cheerful and generous in giving. All giving only returns to our Father what is his.

■ Be sure to financially support your local church as a primary responsibility. International preaching and care support should follow as well.

## DON'T

■ Covet financial blessings others enjoy. "Be content with your wages" is good advice for all.

■ Hold back charity, or be dishonest with the IRS. Some disciples paid with their lives for financial dishonesty (Acts 5). It is hard for a rich man to enter the kingdom of god!

# 20.

# Service in Public Prayer

"O come, let us sing for joy to the Lord, let us shout joyfully to the rock of our salvation."

Ps 95:1

"Lord, teach us to pray" is just as needful and relevant today as it was 2,000 years ago. Can you remember any details from the last prayer you heard in church? Can you remember any details from any public prayer five minutes afterwards? The challenges we all have with private prayer are the same struggles as our public prayers. We tend to fall into repetition and canned phrases that we are familiar with. Most of us know what other brothers will say in their prayers because of unintended repetition. Do we think that God wants to hear the "same-old, same-old" in each of our prayers?

My church has a special time for "prayer for others" during Sunday service. This has become one of the most important times in our service and normally follows the weekly announcements. We ask anyone to submit names and details so that the presider will include each person's need in our public prayer. This has become a huge encouragement for members, and a positive element to share with friends and co-workers when they are in need. This can be a hard job for the presider, but so rewarding to all involved. There were some exceptional public, model prayers in scripture.

Solomon gave a wonderful prayer for the dedication of the temple, which served as a guide to his nation for generations to come (1 Kings 8). Elijah prayed for a miraculous deliverance in his contest with the prophets of Baal. God answered him, and the people of Israel were finally convinced, repeating, "The Lord, He is God." Of course Jesus gave his disciples the model prayer for all time when he guided them, and us, in our prayer life. "Our Father, which art in heaven...."

One refugee brother gave the following prayer in our church during memorial service. Some of our "experienced" brothers could use a refresher course from "babes in Christ" for more effective public prayers like this: "Heavenly Father, we say thank you for this wonderful moment. And we say thank you for your Word that we have received from your worker—to be reminding us about the work of your son Jesus Christ, as a hard worker. The one who has done everything for us as His work. Now we say thank you for this bread, and this wine, to be reminding us of him, as our everything. We say thank you, Lord, in Jesus's name we pray, Amen."

*Don't forget to pray for others outside the church. Use the following tips for guidance.*

## DO

■ Speak loud enough for people to hear and aim to be brief.

■ Pray like Jesus—with sincerity, passion and heart.

■ Be as specific as possible. Overgeneralizing prayers can feel empty.

■ Pray in the name of Jesus or Yeshua (John 14:13).

## DON'T

■ Preach to people. Pray to the Creator of the universe with reverence.

■ Pray with empty phrases or repetitious, churchy words.

■ Assume praying in King James English is more holy than using simple words. God is not impressed with our best vocabulary.

# 21.

# Service by Music
## *The Joy of an Eight-Year-Old*

"I have no greater joy than to hear that my children are walking in the truth."

3 John 4

Music, singing, and dancing are mentioned hundreds of times throughout the Scriptures. Yet despite the numerous commands to "sing to the Lord," I struggle with the importance of music. This may seem odd coming from a music major, but for years I wondered what the true purpose of music is on Sunday mornings. Is it simply to achieve an emotional high? What makes music so special that it's prescribed as a way to express praise and gratitude to our Heavenly Father? Music can transcend our lives, but I found myself experiencing those sublime moments during my music studies as opposed to church settings. At college I was blown away by Bach's brilliance displayed in his Musical Offering, or by the unity and clarity of 200+ voices singing Mozart's Requiem.

On Sundays, however, I almost dreaded accompanying singers who consistently sang out of tune and were unable to sight-read new music. But as I considered joy and the command to "serve the Lord with gladness; come before Him with joyful singing" (Ps. 100:2), my mind turned to a musically-inclined mentor. In talking with him, he mentioned how "the joy of music is experiencing it like an eight-year-old." While joy is often (and correctly) distinguished from the emotion of happiness, God asks for gladness and jubilance when singing His praises. As my mentor described, music is the key to the rarely visited, creative right side of our brain, as we normally entertain the left side of our brain to accomplish logical tasks. Though I had heard (and promptly ignored) this before, I realized that my sacrifice of praise was missing true joy. I was so focused on the grammar of the music that I did not allow it to captivate my heart.

We can spend years aiming to discover the true, important meaning of music in the lives of a believer. However, I believe that this exercise in itself is contrary to God's intent with His gift of music. Each and every one of us can experience music as an eight-year-old does: carefree and with exuberant joy. "Playing skillfully" (Ps. 33:3) is merely a means to an end. One of the goals of music is joy, and we can experience that joy now, in preparation for the joy to come as we sing praises to our Lord and King.

*The following tips will help you experience the full joy of music.*

## DO

■ Sing to the Lord and not to an audience.

■ Practice to develop your musical gifts, or support others.

■ Treat music as praise with proper reverence.

## DON'T

■ Be critical of others who lack musical ability.

■ "Sit on the sidelines" during church hymns.

■ Be embarrassed with the quality of your singing. Musical praise is for our Creator.

# 22.

# Service by Teaching Sunday School

"These words, which I am commanding you today, shall be on your heart. You shall teach them diligently to your sons and shall talk of them when you sit in your house and when you walk by the way and when you lie down and when you rise up."

Deuteronomy 6:6-7

Teaching our young people is a great gift and opportunity towards preaching God's truth. There are many tools and tricks of the trade to help bless and enhance the classroom experience: seasoned veterans, established curriculums, strong spiritual support, ample opportunity to serve, and genuine need. Anyone willing to embrace the world of teaching is looking for inspiration, encouragement, a sense of purpose, and comfort to carry the torch of knowledge closer to applied wisdom. Keep in mind that with every moment you explore, and every treasure you uncover, you are sowing seeds and nurturing their spiritual care for the time of harvest when God will give the increase of everlasting fruit. "It is the glory of God to conceal a matter; to search out a matter is the glory of Kings" (Proverbs 25:2).

With this gift comes great responsibility to the precious little ones we serve (James 3:1). Make your time together an eventful gathering with meaning. Search the scriptures, seek and apply Godly wisdom, make connections with object lessons and everyday items. Embracing and encouraging work in the Lord's true service takes daily commitment and practice. Promoting and inviting a loving attitude for personal study and growth leads to seeking God's Kingdom first. Peer exercises can build strong and lasting relationships within His house-

*Teach young people to be dutiful servants of God with the following guidelines.*

## DO

■ Know, love, and apply your lesson content and material. Your enthusiasm is catching. When you spiritually feed others, you yourself are also refreshed. Good teachers are great students at heart!

■ Make your "gift" relevant; give it with purpose in mind. All good gifts come from above, and bring us closer in our walk to His Kingdom. "For I know the plans I have for you," declares the Lord, "plans to prosper you and not to harm you, plans to give you hope and a future" (Jeremiah 29:11).

■ Live to shake things up in class; don't let your style become so routine that it loses its appeal and zeal.

## DON'T

■ Be shy or afraid to share from personal examples. You may become a lifeline to your students throughout their lives.

■ "Just wing it!" First consider your gift: its recipient, its purpose, and on whose behalf you are presenting it. Go to Him in prayer and with an open mind; He will help you tie His Truth neatly with a bow of divine blessing.

■ Make your lessons all about facts and Bible knowledge, but rather daily application. Help your students to both learn and live the truth.

hold with you as their guide and spiritual guardian. To accomplish so much in under an hour is a real challenge and true calling to make the most of the opportunity, your gifts, and His blessing. Consider what inspires you most so you can in turn share it with others of like precious faith. As you have freely received, also freely give cheerfully for God loves a cheerful giver (2 Corinthians 9:7).

Gifts come in a variety of packaging! Put some time, thought, and detail into your presentation. Don't just wing it, but get creative with some special enhancements and attention-getters. Themes and timelines are valuable resources for establishing classroom structure. Use visual echoes to assist with greater attention, retention, and a genuine zeal for learning. Our minds are designed to respond to games and puzzles (mysteries needing to be searched out and solved), pretty wrappings (engaging and channeling one's focus) and fun "toy" toppers (hands-on application and instruction). The more questions we explore, clues we collect, and seeds we plant, the more faith and truth we inspire with our efforts in such fertile fields. Welcome the investment and service to effectively wrap up your class material as the gift that He intended for His children. When you give, you too will receive. There is much joy to be gleaned in the gift exchange—a compelling and revealing process of true lessons learned—and its shared delivery.

# 23.

# Serving Brother's Responsibilities

"For even the Son of Man did not come to be served, but to serve, and to give his life as a ransom for many."

Mark 10:45

Those who serve as speakers and leaders in the church aspire to a good thing (1 Timothy 3:1) and take on extra responsibility in our lay-ministry faith. Those who lead at church "will be judged more strictly" according to James (3:1). There is much Biblical instruction about how men as leaders answer to a higher calling:

**Old Testament Priestly Leader Requirements**

- Age: Priests (males) could only serve from 30 to 50 years old (Numbers 4)
- Tribe: Priests had to be descended from Levi (Exodus 27:21, 29:44)
- Marriage: Priests could only marry a virgin (Leviticus 21:13-15)
- Alcohol: Not allowed (Leviticus 10:8-10)
- Cleanliness: Priests could not be ceremonially unclean and serve (Leviticus 22:3-8)
- Nazarites: No touching dead bodies, no alcohol, no uncleanness (Numbers 6)
- Defects: No blind or lame or any defect allowed to serve (Leviticus 21:16-18)

### New Testament Male Leaders Responsibilities

- Husband of one wife (1 Timothy 3:2)
- Fathers of obedient children (1 Timothy 3:12, Titus 1:6)
- Not an alcoholic, free from love of money (1 Timothy 3:3)
- Gentle, able to teach, respectable, hospitable (1 Timothy 3:2)
- Above reproach & able to exhort in sound doctrine (Titus 1:7-9)

### Practical Expectations for Brothers as Church Leaders

**1.** Must attend church weekly unless due to illness or unusual circumstances. We're told that we "should not forsake the assembling together" for church (Hebrews 10:25). Attending Memorial Service every week possible should be our obvious conviction. Church members won't respect speakers who don't attend regularly or who skip Sunday school and Bible class.

**2.** Should attend all other church functions including Sunday school and weekly Bible classes. "Set the believers an example" is Paul's advice (1 Tim 4). We each need to be encouraged, and to encourage, more than one hour on Sunday morning.

**3.** Church leaders should be regular readers of God's word. We starve ourselves spiritually when we miss our spiritual meals and therefore can't help others with their needs. We "draw near to God" by reading the Bible, and it shows to others through our words and actions.

**4.** Leaders must be committed to serve. Not just when it's convenient or easy or by choice. Jesus gave his disciples the perfect example, serving those who were foreigners, unclean, crazy, desperate, sick, hungry, despised, and rejected.

# 24.

# Serving Sister's Responsibilities

"Charm is deceitful and beauty is vain, but a woman who fears the LORD, she shall be praised. Give her the product of her hands, and let her works praise her in the gates."

Proverbs 31:30

Sisters are the glue that holds churches together. In fact, many times nothing gets done without women doing the planning and activity. Some sisters are especially endowed with wisdom to help settle divisive problems (2 Sam 14:2; 2 Sam 20:16-22). Other times it is the women who do the heavy lifting with practical acts of kindness. When was the last time a group of men planned and implemented writing cards for the sick or those absent from church? Sisters are uniquely gifted to use compassion and care to help those in need.

**Old Testament Female Responsibilities:**

- Physical labor: Women have historically been just as active as men (Gen 24:11; Ex 2:16)

- Church helpers: Women served at the tabernacle and tent of meeting (Ex 35:25-29; Ex 38:8; 1 Sam 2:22)

- Temple singers: Women shared with men some support roles (Ezra 2:65)

- Support roles: Unlike Miriam, need to be submissive (Numbers 12)

■ Servant maiden: Godly women served others often (1 Sam 25:41-42; 1 Pet 3:6)

### New Testament Female Responsibilities

■ Faithful prophetess (Luke 2:36-38; Acts 21:9)

■ Subject to men (1 Tim 2:11-12; 1 Cor 11:3-10; 1 Cor 14:33-35; 1 Peter 3:5)

■ Be reverent and holy (Titus 2:3-5; 1 Tim 3:11. Prayerful: Acts 1:14; 1 Tim 5:5)

■ Financial & practical caregivers (Matt 27:55; Luke 8:1-3)

■ Deaconess/servants (Rom 16:1-7; Acts 12:2)

■ Co-worker with men (Aquila and Priscilla in Acts 18; Philippians 4:3)

■ Care for family (1 Tim 5:3-8, 14; 1 Thes 2:7; Titus 2:4)

■ Acts of kindness (Luke 7:36-50; Luke 10:38; Tabitha in Acts 9:36)

### Practical Advice for Sisters

**1.** Sisters should model their spiritual lives after maternal Sarah (Heb 11:11), Godly Abigail (1 Sam 25), faithful Rahab (Heb 11:31), serving Mary (Luke 1), thankful Mary Magdalene and other like-minded women of faith.

**2.** Sisters do well to study women of faith and model lives after such examples. The women who followed Jesus and provided for his disciples are wonderful examples (Luke 8:1-3). Sisters need to prioritize their own spiritual lives to be in tune to Jesus first.

**3.** There are many ways sisters can serve within the church. Teaching Sunday school, playing piano, preparing emblems, supporting Bible classes and cooking are just the basics. Wise sisters use gentle words to encourage others, solve problems, give godly advice, and teach all. A faithful sister can have more positive influence than everyone else at church.

**4.** Outside the church there are no limits to helping others. Volunteering for charities that touch the needy, caring for the elderly or including widows in social events, seeking out needs, and sacrificing personal time. Serving sisters make all the difference.

# Part 4

## Service in Sermons

"Then the King will say to those on His right, 'Come, you who are blessed of My Father, inherit the kingdom prepared for you from the foundation of the world. For I was hungry, and you gave Me something to eat; I was thirsty, and you gave Me something to drink; I was a stranger, and you invited Me in; naked, and you clothed Me; I was sick, and you visited Me; I was in prison, and you came to Me.'"

Matthew 25:34-36

# 25.

# Serving by Exhorting *A Message with Meaning*

"Preach the word of God. Be prepared, whether the time is favorable or not. Patiently correct, rebuke, and encourage your people with good teaching." 2 Tim 4:2

Exhortations are not all created equal. The most important aspect of any church speech is the message. It's more important than preparation, delivery, introductions, conclusions, audience involvement, or visual aids. Nothing is more important than the basic message being communicated. Perhaps you have heard a good talk at church, but at the end you really couldn't repeat what the message was to you. Listeners should be able to understand and remember the basic message. This is one of the greatest failings in our exhortations. Speakers need to give clear and simple messages to be effective. Presenters must first focus exhortations on what message needs to be communicated to the audience on that day.

The Bible is full of exceptional speeches. Each one is only meaningful because of the message to the listeners. Think of John the Baptist and how he really was "the voice of one crying in the wilderness." Or Elijah when he challenged Israel by saying, "how long will you go limping with two different opinions?" Elijah objected to the sinful status quo and, with God's help, won over the nation. What about Jonah crying out among the Gentiles, "Yet forty days and Nineveh will be overthrown." Jonah didn't choose his message or his audience, but he left all peoples a timeless lesson in repentance. Or Jesus when he gave the greatest speech ever on the mount in Galilee The result was "they were amazed at his teaching, for His message was with authority."

*If you are a speaker and want to do your best, consider these simple suggestions:*

## DO

■ Ask yourself what basic message you want people to take home. Then pray for guidance and God's blessing that your words are His words.

■ Make sure your message is easy to understand by all, especially young people.

■ Aim for your message to cause action by listeners. Make it relevant today

■ Keep asking yourself, "What is my main message?"

■ Make sure your message connects to Jesus in some way.

## DON'T

■ Talk negatively about other religions or have a negative message.

■ Talk only to mature adults. Teenagers are our future and need your message. Children hear more than we think as well.

■ Talk without having a message. Talk with purpose.

■ Give the same talk every time. Make your messages varied and well rounded.

What will your next message be? Do you tend to speak about the same messages each time you speak? How do you decide what your subject will be? Some messages are better than others, depending on the situation, need and audience. Paul's singular message to the Corinthians was only about "Jesus Christ and him crucified" (1 Cor 2:2). Speakers need to focus on a single message, and the message needs to connect with the audience.

# 26.

# Preparing for Speaking Success

"If anyone speaks, they should do so as one who speaks the very words of God. If anyone serves, they should do so with the strength God provides, so that in all things God may be praised through Jesus Christ."
1 Peter 4:11

A speaker needs to prepare an exhortation with the thought that this will be their best talk yet. Why else waste your time and that of a room full of listeners? Your audience certainly knows how much you prepare for your talks. It is that obvious. Successful speaking groups like Toastmasters emphasize how important preparation is to giving a great talk. You just can't show up and wing it and expect to give your best talk yet. Great talks require serious preparation. That means giving plenty of time preparing an important message and doing enough research.

If possible plan to share a personal story that fits your topic. Stories are often the only thing that your audience will remember from your talk. If you don't have a personal story that fits your subject, go online and find one that does. Sources like SermonCentral.com are helpful for adding colorful content to your talk. Share some humor if appropriate. As speakers, we need to prepare our message so that listeners take action. It should take more than a couple hours to do a thorough job preparing a great exhortation.

Don't you think that Jesus prepared ahead of time before giving the Sermon on the Mount, or various parables? Our Lord was a master speaker, in part, because he meditated on the scriptures in preparation for his lessons. Samuel cried to the Lord all night before delivering a punishing message to King Saul. Esther prepared with

*Church speakers have a high calling and big responsibility to uplift and encourage fellow believers. James (3:1) says that teachers will be judged more strictly. If you want to make your next talk your best yet, consider these hints for preparation:*

## DO

■ Organize your talk logically, make the order easy to follow and understand.

■ Practice your talk and make sure you speak within time limits.

■ Study your content so that your preparation is obvious to the audience.

■ Plan to teach, not just talk. Prepare for what effect you want to have on your audience.

## DON'T

■ Procrastinate preparation. Do not start writing your talk within 48 hours of Sunday.

■ Arrive just in time, plan to be early and plan to stay late to talk afterwards.

■ Write a two-hour talk to deliver in thirty minutes. Plan to end early and talk less.

prayer and fasting before speaking her mind to her king. John the Baptist was the "voice of one crying in the wilderness" with a mission to "prepare to way of the Lord." He must have prepared by studying Isaiah to deliver his fiery speeches. Job declared, "I have prepared my case; I will be proved innocent" (Job 13:18). He listened to his friend's speeches, but prepared with anticipation what he would say when it was his turn.

# 27.

# Delivering Your Message Like a Pro

"For everyone who asks receives; the one who seeks finds; and to the one who knocks, the door will be opened."

Matthew 7:8

Let's face it: very few speakers are naturally charismatic. You can probably think of a few great speakers who were inspiring, captivating, motivating and entertaining. But that's usually just a small minority of all the public speakers you've heard. Giving great exhortations is not innate. It takes hard work and a lot of experience to do the job right. Having the right message, studying well in advance, preparing diligently and having visual aids are all helpful, but may be for naught if the speaker is unable to engage and keep the audience's attention.

It is said that non-verbal communication is the most important way we communicate in person. When speakers exhort, only part of their exhortation is verbal. A major part is in the body language, visual aids, eye contact, tone of voice and gestures. Great speakers use non-verbal cues to deliver their message more effectively.

One young lady led a youth devotion and started by asking a simple question: "When was the first time that you realized that God loves you?" The question was extremely engaging and a wonderful way to begin her subject, but what really made it work was what she did after that. She paused for a very long time and looked intently at each person in the group. After maybe thirty long seconds, she repeated the same probing question. And the same long pause and eye contact. That short devotion was one of the most memorable for all in the discussion group and a great example for how our delivery can make all the difference in our exhortations.

Jesus did something similar when he was cornered about the woman caught in adultery. He was the master at pausing, and then asking an incredible question or making a teaching statement. Jesus left the crowds in awe because they heard him speak as one with authority, and not as their trained teachers. Remember when Jesus read the scroll of Isaiah in the synagogue, rolled it up, sat down, and then said, "Today this scripture has been fulfilled in your hearing." It's no surprise that every eye was glued to hear the carpenter's son. That was the kind of delivery that helped make Jesus's messages so meaningful.

*Give your next exhortation with ease with the following tips.*

## DO

- Ask probing questions, and repeat your main message.
- Pause. This can be one of your most effective speaking tools.
- Smile during your talk. People want to hear an upbeat message more than a downer.
- Speak with passion and meaning, your subject should be a matter of life and death.

## DON'T

- Read your talk, no great speaker reads their talk word-for-word.
- Make excuses about not being a good speaker, or this not being a good talk, or no one will want to listen.
- Talk too fast or read in a monotone. To be heard, you must engage people to listen.

# 28.

# Engaging Questions

"The conclusion, when all has been heard, is: fear God and keep His commandments, because this applies to every person."

Ecclesiastes 12:13

When did you first realize that God was calling you? Do you believe you have a personal guardian angel? What will really happen on the day Jesus returns? What job do you want to do in the kingdom? Questions like these are great prompts for bible studies and as part of exhortations. This part of communication tends to cause listeners to be more active than passive. And that makes for a better environment for learning and applying. It all starts with engaging questions.

Asking questions during personal bible study is a healthy curiosity. It leads people to study further to answer the "how's" and "why's" of the story. It's a good bible study habit to ask questions about each passage you read. What is the context? What is the history behind the characters? What does this remind me of in other parts of the Bible? Why was this section of the Bible included? How do these verses point to Jesus? What is the lesson for me? These are the types of questions that help disciples become more like Jesus.

The Bible is jam-packed full of questions. The serpent was the first to pose a question (Gen 3:1), but the Creator trumped that when He asked Adam, "Where are you?" God did not ask that question because He didn't know the answer, but as a way to teach Adam. The Lord continued asking more questions to Adam, and then to Eve, as a way to encourage their confession and obedience.

Jesus was a master at asking questions as a way to teach. Consider these examples from Matthew alone: "Do you believe that I am able to do this? What did you go out into the wilderness to see? A reed swayed by the wind? If not, what did you go out to see? A man dressed in fine clothes? To what can I compare this generation? Do you believe that I am able to do this? Who do people say that the Son of Man is? But what about you? Who do you say that I am? Are you able to drink the cup that I will drink? What do you think about the Messiah? Whose son is he?"

*Jesus always seemed to teach using the right question at the right time. If we want to be like him, we will too. Use the following tips to help you find the right questions.*

## DO

■ Plan to use questions during talks, even rhetorical questions gain attention. Some speakers use questions to spark audience participation, be willing to entertain questions or comments if you do.

■ Ask open-ended questions that lead to the answer you want.

■ Use gestures as part of questions, such as raising your own arm as an example.

## DON'T

■ Ask too obvious questions such as "Who created Adam and Eve?" Aim to challenge and engage listeners.

■ Forget to ask how your subject relates to Jesus. Make them think.

■ Let your audience get too comfortable. Ask uncomfortable questions. Isn't that what Jesus did?

# 29.

# Attention-Getting Introductions and Vivid Conclusions

"For the word of the cross is foolishness to those who are perishing, but to us who are being saved it is the power of God."

1 Corinthians 1:18

Boom. Thirty seconds. That's the amount of time speakers have to set the tone, connect to their audience and make sure people will keep listening. First impressions matter. Failure to deliver a great opening means that many will tune out before even hearing your message. You can't just put the burden on the audience and expect them to listen regardless of your delivery. You need to grab their attention in a memorable way, since the introduction needs to be something special.

Jesus set the bar for introductions very high when he read from Isaiah and said, "Today this scripture has been fulfilled in your hearing." Every eye in that synagogue was glued to Jesus and locked in to every word he spoke. Paul gave a stunning opening to his speech to the Jewish Council when he said, "Brethren, I have lived my life with a perfectly good conscience before God up to this day"(Acts 23:1). That shocking introduction prepared his message for its full effect. John thc Baptist started his message to the crowds, "You brood of vipers! Who warned you to flee from the coming wrath?" John preached about repentance and used his introduction to get people's attention.

In the Old Testament, Job had a series of back-and-forth speeches with his three supposed friends. For an interesting study, read the first two verses of each chapter in Job starting in Chapter 3. You'll notice that Job and his friends make some pretty incredible introductions, and these tend to be summaries of the message to follow:

- "Does God pervert justice? Does the Almighty pervert what is right?" (8:3)

*Follow the tips below when devising an attention-getting introduction.*

## DO

- Invest your preparation time.

- A good story is usually a helpful introduction, make sure it leads to your subject.

- Make sure your conclusion leaves the memory you want. Consider ending by reading a verse to let God have the last word. Be sure your conclusion has a tie in to Jesus for the breaking of bread.

## DON'T

- Think your preparation is over until you have a winning introduction and conclusion.

- Settle for a boring introduction, or worse, none at all.

- Introduce new thoughts in your conclusion; it should be a summary.

- "How can mere mortals prove their innocence before God?" (9:1)

- "I have heard many such things, miserable comforters are you all." (16:1)

- "How long will you torment my soul? And break me in pieces with words." (19:1)

- "Can a man be of benefit to God?" (22:1)

- "But now they mock me, men younger than I." (30:1)

# 30.

# PowerPoint and Visual Aids

"He was oppressed and He was afflicted, Yet He did not open His mouth; Like a lamb that is led to slaughter, And like a sheep that is silent before its shearers, So He did not open His mouth."

Isaiah 53:7

A visiting speaker led a study weekend and many years later only one thing is memorable. The speaker intentionally and loudly broke a plate to make a point. Unfortunately, it's likely that no one in the audience remembers the subject or lesson from that attention-getting trick. That's the challenge with visual aids. Speakers need to make sure that visual aids, including PowerPoint, add to the main message and don't distract in any way. A map, electronic media, flip chart, physical object or other visual aid can powerfully connect the audience with the speaker and greatly improve recall. The challenge and opportunity for speakers is to make visual aids work.

One brother gave a talk on "Home in Christ" and started with a demonstration using a deck of cards. He asked someone from the audience to come forward and show how to build a "house" with playing cards. The object lesson hit the mark as the message connected the visual aid with the lesson. Like many prophets, Jeremiah acted out an object lesson when he was told to go and watch the potter work with clay (Jeremiah 18). He used that visual aid to dramatically drive home the same point he had been making for years. That's how visual aids should work.

Can you recall when Jesus used visual aids as part of his public talks? Jesus was a master storyteller who used parables as the visual aid of his day. He spoke about a man who had a log in his eye and compared him to another who only had a speck in his. Jesus gave object lessons using a mustard seed, a sower and his seed, patching new vs. old garments, a denarius coin, fruit from fig trees and physically washing feet. At the Last Supper Jesus instituted a repetitive object lesson that his disciples followed. The symbols of bread and wine still affect believers today.

One final thought. Please don't hesitate to ask for help with your PowerPoint presentations. There are many skills and tricks to making a really effective presentation. Take mental notes next time you watch a good PowerPoint presentation and plan to make your next visual aid your best yet.

*Take the time necessary to prepare a great PowerPoint presentation with help from the pointers below.*

## DO

■ If you use PowerPoint, do it right. Don't read long slides, and learn how to include great full-screen photos. A picture really is worth a thousand words.

■ Make sure your visual aid leaves a positive, lasting impression that supports your main message.

■ Consider using an object lesson to help people connect and remember. The extra effort is worth it.

## DON'T

■ Spend ten hours preparation time on PowerPoint and only one hour on content. Visual aids do not replace the message.

■ Fill PowerPoint with full-page quotes in small font size. Do limit lines per page.

# 31.

# Exhorting Without Words

"Therefore, I exhort the elders among you, as your fellow elder and witness of the sufferings of Christ... shepherd the flock of God among you.... according to the will of God."

1 Peter 5:1-2

Speakers communicate more when they don't use words! Stanford's researcher Albert Mehrabian demonstrated that 55 percent of all understanding received in lectures comes from the speaker's body language. 38 percent of communication comes from voice tone and only 7 percent comes from actual word content. How can this be possible? Think about any poor talk you have heard and how it was communicated non-verbally. Did the speaker put his hands in his pockets? Did he look down at his words and just read his talk? Did he seem bored himself? Or unhappy? Positive communication without words is essential to deliver your intended message.

We can learn much from watching TV evangelists. These professionals almost never stand behind a pulpit because they know this puts a barrier between them and the audience. A pulpit really is a speaker's crutch and not helpful for delivering an effective talk. Watch a religious service on TV with the sound off and note the body language and physical activity. Pros know how important it is to communicate in various forms. They are experts at using every teaching trick to keep the audience engaged and actively listening.

Jesus often spoke volumes without speaking. When the woman caught in adultery was placed before him, he chose to bend down and silently write on the ground. He walked on the Sea of Galilee, intending to go past his disciples without any interaction. Jesus had compassion on the multitudes. Some people brought babies so that he would touch them, not to hear his words. In Jesus' last hours, "the Lord turned and looked at Peter" after his third denial. His scanning look was more than enough to communicate his thoughts. Jesus also chose not to speak to Pilate or Herod, so that they were quite amazed. He could have spoken to Herod, especially, but instead his actions spoke louder than his words.

*If you want to exhort like Jesus, consider some tips below.*

## DO

■ Aim to go out of your comfort zone with your hands, feet, posture and gestures. Be aware how important your non-verbal communication really is.

■ Make sure you look people in the eye; this is critical to connect with your audience. Don't forget to smile and be welcoming to all.

■ Consider use of a physical object lesson, it will be memorable.

## DON'T

■ Put your hands in your pockets. Only bad things follow.

■ Write (and read) your talk on full pages, it's distracting to see a speaker fiddle with pages. Use note cards.

■ Forget that your body language may be just as important as your message! People subconsciously "read" your non-verbal communication as much as your intended message.

# 32.

# Presiding with Passion

"For I received from the Lord that which I also delivered to you, that the Lord Jesus in the night in which He was betrayed took bread."

1 Corinthians 11:23

The role of the presider, or president/chairman in some countries, cannot be underestimated. He has the primary responsibility to set the spiritual tone for the day. His job can literally make a difference whether listeners go home properly filled. It's certainly not an easy job. Many speakers would say that it is much harder than speaking, particularly for younger brothers. It takes a lot of practice, effort and experience to do the job right. And it can be a blessing to all who attend your service.

A presider needs to be just as organized as the speaker. He needs to prepare comments ahead of time, arrive early and plan to stay late. The presider should try to be a welcoming person, personally talking to visitors, if possible, and making all feel comfortable and appreciated for attending. Perhaps you can recall a presider who noticeably does a great job. Be sure to thank him for his role in making that service a spiritual success.

Can you think of any "presider" types in the Bible? Aaron and Moses split roles for being the main speaker and support person. Aaron seemed to be the natural speaker and Moses perhaps more like our presider role at times. John the Baptist was a presider in the sense that he "prepared the way of the Lord." Our presider job is similar in that he should prepare the audience for the one to come, and later connect comments to Messiah. Barnabas was another presider-type, who partnered with Paul, the chief speaker. Each secondary speaker, or presider, in the Bible plays a vital role for communicating the gospel message.

Presiders "set the table" for the service to be effective. A spiritual brother who presides well really helps the flow of the meeting. He needs to be able to make good decisions when something goes wrong too. God willing, surprises will be few! Pray before you begin that you may honor your heavenly Father and serve in a Christ-like manner.

*If you are a presider at church, and want to do your best, consider the suggestions below.*

## DO

- Prepare to preside like an exhortation. Be organized and use few words.
- Read the Word of God with emotion and sincerity, not in a monotone.
- Repeat hymn numbers and readings two or three times each minimum.
- Prepare yourself spiritually before the service. You need to feel spiritually in tune with Jesus in order to serve others.

## DON'T

- Rush the service, but don't be too slow either. Either way can be a distraction for the audience.
- Assume presiding is unimportant. It's actually really important.
- Repeat the exhortation or give a second talk yourself.

# 33.

# Memorial Service

"The Lord Jesus, on the night he was betrayed, took bread, and when he had given thanks ,he broke it and said, 'This is my body, which is for you; do this in remembrance of me. In the same way, after supper he took the cup, saying, 'This cup is the new covenant in my blood; do this whenever you drink it, in remembrance of me.'"

1 Corinthians 11:24

Sometimes we forget that Jesus was the presider at the first Memorial Service. He gathered his disciples in the upper room that evening because he earnestly desired to share the Passover meal together. Jesus used his words sparingly that night, as his actions spoke volumes. He washed his disciples' feet. He broke the bread and shared the wine. When he spoke, his disciples listened. Lives were changed, and the apostles never forgot that night or the things Jesus said. Jesus set the standard for presiding brothers to follow.

Presiding over the Memorial Service is a difficult task. It requires quick thinking to help transition the service from the exhortation to communion. Depending on the exhortation subject, this can be challenging. Yet Presiders have a great responsibility to help prepare the members spiritual frame of mind. We tend to read the same passages every week. Matthew 26, Luke 22, John 6, 1 Corinthians 11, Isaiah 53, and Psalm 22 come to mind. It is a challenge to not fall into a rut and read and repeat the same words every Sunday. There are a full range of scriptures to draw from to help members think more about Jesus and his sacrifice.

"This is my body. This is my blood. Do this in remembrance of me." These are relatively simple words and yet deeply intriguing, inspiring and compelling. Presiders have the job of motivating fellow

*Successfully exhort at your next Memorial Service with the following pointers.*

## DO

■ Do your best to tie the exhortation to the essence of the Memorial Service.

■ Include different memorial readings to help keep a fresh perspective.

■ Keep the focus on Jesus. He is our savior, He is our master. Ask yourself how your words can help the spiritual life and renewal for all in your meeting.

## DON'T

■ Talk more than five to seven minutes; keep the focus on the breaking of bread.

■ Repeat the exhortation, that only takes away from the speaker.

■ Talk about Jesus being our brother. That may be true, but He should be elevated far above all rule and authority, power, dominion and every name in all ages, in our thinking and words (Ephesians 1:21).

■ Whisper when handing out the memorials. Speak so all can hear or don't speak at all.

disciples to remember Jesus, and to act more like Him. This is the time to connect the bread to Jesus body, and the wine to His blood. This is the time to remind all that this service is for the forgiveness of their sins.

The seriousness of breaking bread in memory of Jesus is unique in Christian discipleship. This is the time when we draw near to The Cross. The Upper Room. The Last Supper. The Garden of Gethsemane. The Bread of Life. The Trial. The Way, The Truth and The Life. Our Sinfulness. His Passion. The King of Israel. This is when we draw near to the Son of God, who died and gave his life for me.

# Conclusion

"Remember me for this, my God, and do not blot out what I have so faithfully done for the house of my God and its services."
Nehemiah 13:14

Now what will you do? Will any of these tips help you to be a more effective servant? My hope and prayer is that these brief thoughts will encourage you to be a better disciple of Jesus Christ. We know that good works will not save us (2 Tim 1:9; Matt 7:21-23; Rev 2:19-21), but doing good deeds should flow naturally from our faith. Jesus challenged His followers in many ways. In the book of Revelation alone, Jesus taught, reminded, and encouraged disciples to serve others through good works.

If you really want to apply lessons here in your life, then start making your own "to-do" list. People who get things done don't leave actions to chance. They make a list and then start working on one item at a time. If you really want to accomplish something, write it down. It shows serious intent and acts as a reminder to help you do what you want to do. If you really want to be more like Jesus, then start writing down actions that you feel called to do. You might not change the world overnight, but if you can help even one person today, then you made a difference. As Mother Teresa once said, "If you can't feed one hundred people, then feed just one."

# About the Author

*Dan Richard* is a lifelong Bible student. He actively seeks to put his faith into action and this short volume is a result of extensive dealings with refugees. Dan is a lay minister and also works full time as the sales and marketing head of NOW Foods, a large family-owned nutrition company.

He has previously written three books including *Beating the Odds,* a history book about NOW. He also wrote *Operation Lost Sheep,* which encourages Christians to search and rescue those who have left the church. Dan and his wife Beth live in Carol Stream, IL.

# Index